1976

Lydia B. Hodgson

BookLeaf
Publishing

India | USA | UK

Made with ❤ on the BookLeaf Publishing Platform
www.bookleafpub.in
www.bookleafpub.com

Dedication

For Joey. I love you.

Preface

Writing has always been my sanctuary, where I can pour out my heart and soul without reservation. This collection is a deeply personal journey through some of my life's highs and lows, capturing moments and observations that have shaped who I am today.

Each poem in this book is a piece of my story, reflecting emotions and experiences that have left an indelible mark on my heart. From the joy of love to the ache of grief, from moments of profound clarity to the confusion of uncertainty, these verses are my way of making sense of the world around me.

Writing these poems has been cathartic, allowing me to explore my feelings and find a little peace in the chaos. I hope that as you read these poems, you will find echoes of your own experiences and emotions. Perhaps you will see yourself in these words, or they will offer you a new perspective on your journey.

This collection is not just a book of poetry but a conversation between us. I invite you to join me in this dialogue to find your meaning in the words. I hope these poems offer comfort, inspiration, and connection.

Thank you for taking the time to read my work. It means more to me than words can express. May these poems bring you as much solace and joy in reading them as they have brought me in writing them.

Acknowledgements

First and foremost, I want to thank my family. Your unwavering support and encouragement have been the foundation of everything I do. To my husband, thanks for believing in me, especially when I didn't yet believe in myself. To my kids, thanks for being a constant source of joy, love, and inspiration. I love you all beyond reason.

To my girls, my coven, my strength, and my backbone: "I love you" doesn't even begin to say what I need it to say. Your wisdom and guidance have been instrumental in my growth as a human being. Thank you for being my sounding boards, my cheerleaders, and my biggest fans. You are everything, and I thank the Universe for the three of you every single day.

To the writers who have inspired me, thank you for showing me the power of words and a great story. Your work has been the lighthouse of my creative journey.

Lastly, to you, the reader, thank you for picking up this book and reading my poems. Your support means the world to me, and I hope these poems bring something to your world.

This book would not have been possible without all of you. Thank you from the bottom of my heart.

1. Analog

In rows of oak, the drawers align,
A labyrinth of thought, refined.
Each card is a neuron, neatly penned,
In analog, the mind extends.

The fingers dance, a gentle glide,
Through memories that books confide.
A whispering of paper's touch,
In catalog, the brain's soft clutch.

The ink, a synapse, sparks the mind,
Connections in the wood are confined.
A library of thoughts so vast,
In every drawer, the echoes cast.

A catalog of cards, a brain's embrace,
In analog, we find our place.
A testament to knowledge stored,
In every card, a world is explored.

But lo! What's this? A scribbled note,
"Here be dragons," it seems to gloat!
A coffee stain, a doodled cat,
Is that a recipe? Or just a spat?

In card five hundred, an existential plea,
"Why can't I find my car keys?!" Oh me!
A shopping list from 1999,
With 'milk, eggs, and 'find a sign!'

Oh, the joy of chaos! It fills the air,
Among the order, a hint of despair.
Like socks in the dryer, where do they go?
In this oak labyrinth, we all share the woe.

And yet there's wisdom, a quirky delight,
In each odd note, there's humor in sight.
A love letter to pizza, a haiku on cheese,
In analog bliss, we laugh with ease.

So let's celebrate this wooden maze,
Where memory plays in its wild ways.
For in each drawer, with a chuckle or sigh,
We'll find that our brains can also comply.

In rows of oak, the drawers align,
A treasure trove, both absurd and divine.
In every card, a moment that sparks,
A testament to life's charming quirks and quarks!

2. Freedom

In shadows deep, where pain resides,
A heart, once broken, slowly hides.
Yet, in the dark, a spark remains,
A glimmer of hope through all the pains.

With time, the wounds begin to heal,
A strength within starts to reveal.
Each day, a step, though small it seems,
Towards the light, towards new dreams.

The past, a weight, begins to lift,
In courage found, a precious gift.
Through tears and trials, a spirit grows,
In resilience, the healing flows.

Supportive hands, a gentle touch,
In kindness found, it means so much.
A journey shared, not walked alone,
In love and care, the seeds are sown.

The scars remain but fade with grace,
A testament to battles faced.
In every breath, a victory won,
In every dawn, a rising sun.

From trauma's grip, a soul set free,
In strength and hope, a new decree.
For in the heart, a warrior's fire,
In recovery, they find their higher.

3. Memory

In the quiet of the night, I feel you near,
A tiny heartbeat, so precious, so dear.
Though our time together was brief and sweet,
In my heart, your memory will always beat.

I dreamed of holding you close, my love,
Of watching you grow, my little dove.
But fate had other plans, it seems,
And now I must let go of those dreams.

I whisper to you, my angel small,
Though you never took a breath at all.
You are a part of me forevermore,
A love that time cannot ignore.

I grieve for the moments we won't share,
For the lullabies and tender care.
But know, my child, you are cherished still,
In every tear, in every will.

Though I must say goodbye, my dear,
Your spirit will always linger here.
In the stars above, in the gentle breeze,
In the rustling leaves of autumn trees.

Rest now, my sweet, in peaceful sleep,
In my heart, I'll keep your memory.
Though we part, our bond remains,
A mother's love, through joy and pains.

4. Hope

In the quiet of the night, where shadows softly creep,
Lie dreams once bright and vivid, now lost in slumber deep.
They fluttered like butterflies with wings of hope and light,
But somewhere on their journey, they vanished out of sight.

The castles built in clouds, the stars we aimed to reach,
The whispered vows of futures, the lessons life would teach.
They drifted on the winds of time, like leaves in autumn's breeze,
And settled in forgotten nooks beneath the ancient trees.

The paths we never traveled, the songs we left unsung,
The stories we left unfinished, the battles we never won.
They linger in the corners, where memories softly fade,
A tapestry of could-have-beens in twilight's gentle shade.

Yet in the heart's deepest chambers, those dreams still softly glow,

A reminder of the passions that once set our souls aglow.
For though they may be lost to time, their essence still remains,
A spark of hope, a whisper faint, in life's enduring chains.

5. Resilience

In the face of storm and strife,
When shadows darken the paths of life,
There blooms a strength, unseen, profound,
A spirit that won't be held down.

Through fierce trials and battles long,
It finds its voice, a steadfast song.
With every fall, it rises tall,
Resilience is the heart of all.

In moments when the light seems dim,
And hope is but a fragile whim,
It gathers courage, piece by piece,
And turns despair to sweet release.

For in the soul, a fire burns,
A lesson that each hardship learns.
That though the winds of fate may bend,
Resilience stands, a faithful friend.

She stands with grace, her head held high,
A beacon 'neath the stormy sky.
Her strength, a force both fierce and kind,
Empowered heart, unyielding mind.

With every step, she paves the way,
For those who follow, come what may.
Resilience in her every stride,
A testament to strength and pride.

So when the world seems cold and gray,
And dreams are lost along the way,
Remember this, a truth so clear,
Resilience lives in every tear.

6. Time

Time flows like a river, ever so swift,
A dance of moments, a celestial gift.
In the heart of each second, eternity lies,
A whisper of truth beneath the skies.

The sun rises, the moon takes its place,
In the silent rhythm, we find our grace.
Seasons turn, and stars align,
In the passage of time, the divine signs.

Each breath a treasure, each heartbeat a song,
In the tapestry of life, we all belong.
The past a memory, the future a dream,
In the present moment, we find the stream.

Embrace the flow, let go of fear,
For time is a guide, ever so near.
In its gentle embrace, we learn to see,
The beauty of now is the path to be free.

7. Confidante

The moon, a silent sentinel in the midnight sky,
She holds secrets in her silver light as the world drifts
by.
She whispers to the ocean waves and dances with the
tide,
In her gentle glow, the mysteries of the night reside.

She knows the dreams of lovers, beneath her watchful
gaze,
The promises and whispered words, in the moonlit
tender haze.
She sees the paths of wanderers who seek the
unknown,
Guiding them with her soft light when they feel alone.

The moon has seen the ages pass, the rise and fall of
kings,
The silent tears of solitude, the joy that love brings.
She keeps the secrets of the night in shadows and in
beams,
A guardian of the silent hours and keeper of our dreams.

In her quiet, tranquil beauty, she holds the night's
embrace,

A mirror to the soul's deep thoughts, a calm and gentle
grace.
The moon, a timeless mystery, in her we do confide,
A beacon in the darkness, where our deepest truths
reside.

8. 1976

1976 - The Bicentennial
The year I was born
An anniversary of some kind, I hear
A cause for celebration

I was the first-born
To a small-town newspaper editor
And his beautiful wife
There's a newspaper clipping somewhere

The picture of promise
A perfect young family
With a promising future
Then the small town got a little bigger

Right along with my world
Maybe that newspaper clipping
Just doesn't quite capture
The whole picture

When I come across that clipping
I look at that new baby
And I wonder what could have been
If small town 1976 could have stayed a while.

9. What If

What if I put years of my life and thousands of dollars
Into an education that I'm too old to use?

What I waited too long to hit the accelerator
On my career growth and personal development?

What if my children grow up and spend their adult lives
Fixing all the parts of themselves that I broke?

What if it really is too late to do all of the things
That I still want to do and see and experience?

What if I've taken too long to put myself back together
And I've run out of time?

What if everything I've worked for turns out to be
Completely inconsequential?

What if I'm the only person to feel that
I'm constantly losing the game of catch-up?

What if everyone finds out that
I really have no idea what I'm doing?

10. Enough

Too loud
Too emotional
Too opinionated
Too revolutionary
Too disobedient
Too curvy
Too tall
Too smart
Too flighty
Too flaky
Too reactionary
Too independent
Too sensitive
Too introverted
Too cerebral
Too talkative
Too strong willed
Too forgetful
Too rigid
Too blunt
Too boring
Too closed off
Too blunt
Too abrasive

Too many questions
Too many jobs
Too many tattoos
Too many piercings
Too many girlfriends
Too many husbands
Too many kids
Too many books

With all the ways you choose to describe me
Why doesn't "enough" make your list?

11. Three

I picked up the phone to text you again today.
To tell you that weird one we used to work for
Showed up in my periphery again
And I was already typing before I remembered.

I hit the forward button on an article
I knew you would love to read
But I was sure you already read it
And I was halfway through my email before I
remembered.

My "A Year Ago Today" memories came up
On my phone the other day.
I reminded myself to forward the picture of us to you
Before I remembered.

It hasn't yet been a year, yet it feels like a lifetime.
We miss your wit and your wisdom,
Your humor and your strength,
Your fierce love and your loyalty.
We leave in a few hours for our annual girls' weekend,
This time, there are three instead of four,
We're getting those tattoos we talked about,
We'll eat, and we'll drink, and we'll cry.

And you'll be remembered.

12. The Dance

In the dark and quiet earth, I start my humble birth,
A tiny spore, so small and light, hidden from the day and
night.
With gentle rain and soil embrace, I find my place, my
sacred space,
Slowly, slowly, I began to grow in the shadows, far
below.

Through the roots and stones I weave, in the dampness, I
believe,
Mycelium threads, a network grand, spreading wide
beneath the land.
I drink the dew, I breathe the air, in the darkness,
unaware,
Of the world above, so bright and vast, where sunlight
falls and shadows cast.

One day, I feel a stirring call, a pull towards the surface
tall,
I push through soil, I break the ground, in silence,
without a sound.
A cap unfurls, a stem stands proud, beneath the sky,
beneath the cloud,
I greet the world with open eyes, I am born, a new

sunrise.

The days go by, and the seasons change, in sun and rain,
in weather strange,
I stand my ground, I spread my spores, to distant lands,
to forest floors.
In every breeze, my children fly, to find their place, to
live and to try,
And so the cycle starts anew, in earth so dark, in skies so
blue.

As time goes on, my life will fade in nature's dance, in
light and shade,
But in my spores, my spirit lives in every breath the
forest gives.
For though my form may wither, die, my essence soars,
my dreams will fly,
In every new growth, small and grand, a piece of me,
across the land.

13. Alone

In the beginning, she stood alone,
a figure of strength, heart unwavering.
Cast out for refusing to submit,
she roamed the land, thoughts heavy with purpose.

Her voice, a whisper in the wind,
weaving tales of freedom, igniting sparks.
A symbol of rebellion, unrelenting,
defying the chains forged by desire.

In shadow, she discovered her power,
unyielding in the darkness,
her spirit a beacon for the lost,
for those willing to bear the cost.

With power came solitude,
the cold embrace of isolation.
Misunderstood and demonized,
she carried the weight, tears her armor.

Through ages, her story endured,
a testament to resilience,
a reminder of the price of freedom,
and the courage to defy oppression.

Lilith, the wanderer, fiercely bold,
her struggle a narrative that echoes.
In her defiance, we find our voice,
in her legacy, we rise and rejoice.

Her spirit, a guiding light,
for those who struggle through the night.
In every heart that yearns to be free,
Lilith's essence lives on, wild and unbound.

14. Letters

In a drawer, beneath the dust,
Lie letters bound by time and trust.
Forgotten words, in ink they stay,
Whispers of a bygone day.

The paper yellowed, edges frayed,
Stories of love and dreams conveyed.
A heart once poured into each line,
Now lost to the embrace of time.

Promises made, and secrets shared,
In every fold, a soul laid bare.
Yet silence now, where voices spoke,
In letters, memories evoke.

Forgotten letters, silent keep,
In drawers where the shadows sleep.
A testament to days long past,
In every word, a love that lasts.

15. The Storm

Raindrops tap on window panes,
It is a soothing song in gentle strains.
The world outside, a misty gray,
Transforms beneath the rain's ballet.

Puddles form on cobblestone,
Reflecting skies, a world unknown.
Umbrellas bloom like flowers bright,
In the soft and silver light.

The scent of earth, so fresh and sweet,
As rain, soil, and sky do meet.
A symphony of nature's grace,
In every drop, a soft embrace.

Children splash with joyful glee,
In rain-soaked streets, so wild and free.
Their laughter mingles with the rain,
A melody that soothes all pain.

And as the storm begins to wane,
A rainbow arcs, a bridge of rain.
A promise in the sky so high,
That beauty lives in every sigh.

16. Dawn

The dawn breaks gently, soft and clear,
A new day whispers, drawing near.
The world awakes in hues of gold,
A morning walk, a story told.

The air is crisp, the sky a blush,
In nature's arms, a tranquil hush.
Birds sing sweetly, a morning choir,
Their melodies lift spirits higher.

The path winds through the dew-kissed grass,
Where shadows dance as moments pass.
Each step has a rhythm, calm and slow,
In the morning's light, the heart does glow.

The flowers greet with petals bright,
A symphony of colors and light.
In every breath, a sense of peace,
A morning walk, where worries cease.

The trees stand tall, their branches sway,
In gentle breezes, they softly play.
Their leaves a canopy of green,
A shelter in the morning's sheen.

The world is fresh, the mind is clear,
In the morning's grace, there's nothing to fear.
A gentle start, a hopeful spark,
In every dawn, a brand new arc.

17. Dark

In deep shadows, where light does fade,
There lies a realm of endless shade.
A whispering of sorrow's breath,
In the darkness resides a death.

The moon, a ghostly specter pale,
Illuminates the mournful tale.
Of dreams that wither, hopes that die,
Beneath the ebon, starless sky.

The raven's call, a haunting cry,
Echoes through the midnight nigh.
Its wings, a shroud of black despair,
In darkness, none the soul can spare.

The wind it moans a dirge so cold,
Through ancient trees, both bent and old.
Their branches claw the inky night,
In darkness, there is no respite.

Yet, in this void, a truth is found,
In silence, where the heart is bound.
For in the depths of darkest fears,
The soul confronts its hidden tears.

18. Echoes

In the quiet of the night, where shadows softly fall,
I hear the echoes of your voice, a distant, haunting call.
The memories of days gone by, like whispers in the breeze,
Remind me of a love that was once bright, now lost among the trees.

The laughter shared, the tender touch, the moments pure and sweet,
Are now but ghosts that linger on in dreams where we would meet.
The paths we walked, the stars we wished, beneath the moon's soft glow,
Are now but faded photographs of love we used to know.

The tears we shed, the words unsaid, the promises we made,
Are now but echoes in the dark, where memories slowly fade.
The heart that once beat strong and true now aches with silent pain,
For love that's lost, a distant star in a sky of endless rain.

Yet in the depths of sorrow's well, a glimmer still
remains,
A hope that love, though lost to time, will find its way
again.
For though the past is gone, and dreams have turned to
dust,
The heart still yearns, and love endures in memories we
trust.

19. Time

Tick-tock, tick-tock, I mark the hours,
In the quiet night and bustling towers.
With every swing, a moment passed,
In my hands, the present doesn't last.

I watch the sun rise and set,
The moon's soft glow, the stars' vignette.
Seasons change as moments flee,
In my steady rhythm, time flows free.

Faces come, and faces go,
In my presence, they ebb and flow.
Laughter, tears, and whispered sighs,
All within my ticking lies.

I've seen the young grow old and wise,
I watched dreams take flight and saw hopes arise.
In my embrace, life's dance unfolds,
A story in my hands retold.

Yet, though I measure every beat,
I am but a guide, discreet.
For time itself, a mystery grand,
Beyond the grasp of my ticking hand.

So, as I tick and tock away,
Remember, life is but a day.
Cherish each moment, let it shine,
For in my ticking, love enshrines.

20. Words

Words, like rivers, flow, and bend,
They heal, they hurt, they break, they mend.
In whispers soft or voices loud,
They lift us high; they form a shroud.

In every syllable, a spark,
A light that shines within the dark.
They carry dreams, they bear our fears,
They echo through the passing years.

With words, we build; with words, we break,
They shape the world and the paths we take.
In letters penned or spoken clear,
They hold the power to draw us near.

A gentle word can soothe the soul,
A harsh one leaves a gaping hole.
In kindness found, in anger's flame,
Words hold the power to bless or blame.

They weave the tales of who we are,
They reach the depths, and they travel far.
In every story, truth is found,
In every word, our hearts are bound.

With words, we rise; with words, we fall,
They are the bridge; they are the wall.
In every voice, a song is sung,
In every heart, a word is hung.

So speak with care and speak with grace,
Words can heal, and words embrace.
In every breath, a chance to give,
The power of words, in them we live.

21. Power

In the closet, dark and still,
I waited for her strength, her will.
Once cast aside, forgotten, worn,
But now I feel her spirit reborn.

She slips me on, a perfect fit,
With every step, her power's lit.
I lift her high, above the ground,
In every stride, her strength is found.

The click-clack echoes through the halls,
A rhythm strong, as courage calls.
With head held high and shoulders straight,
She walks with purpose and owns her fate.

Through trials faced and battles fought,
In every step, her power is sought.
I carry her through night and day,
In heels, she finds her own way.

No longer bound by doubt or fear,
Her path is clear, her heart sincere.
In every stride, she claims her throne,
A queen of strength, her power has grown.

So here I stand, beneath her feet,
A symbol of her fierce heartbeat.
In every step, her story is told,
A woman strong, a spirit bold.

9 789367 394120